CAROL'S CORNER

Poems and Inspirational Writings

Carol Alexander-Morgan

Positive Works, LLC
Twinsburg, OH
September 23, 2019

Carol Alexander-Morgan Copyright © 2019
Stripped Naked Manuscript Copyright © 2001 by Library of Congress, Washington D.C.

All rights reserved. No portion of this book may be reproduced, stored in a retrieval system, or transmitted in any form or by any means – electronic, mechanical, photocopy or other – except for brief quotations without the prior written permission of the publisher.

Published by Positive Works, LLC
Twinsburg, OH
Editing by Positive Works, LLC

ISBN: 9781695825123

TABLE OF CONTENTS

Dedication 3

Foreword 4

The Lord's Prayer 5

Prologue 6

PART 1
Love Relationships 7

PART 2
Relationship With God 30

PART 3
Family 47

PART 4
Country 70

DEDICATION

My first book is dedicated to my first born, and only daughter, Michelle.

Remembering you always and loving you even more,

Mom

FOREWORD

Carol and I met many years ago in Cleveland, Ohio. Our paths crossed various times at her family gatherings. Carol was my neighbor's aunt.

As time moved on, so did many of our friends and family members. We have used this time of reconnection to become more deeply acquainted with each other and share in the blessings of aging gracefully during life lessons.

It is never too late to fulfill a lifelong dream. Carol has wanted to publish her poems and writings for many years. You are about to travel in time and through the emotions of Carol's Corner! She has penned thoughts that are precious to her. She has opened her heart to her readers.

Carol sent a card that stated she was glad I came into her life…maybe she should send God a "thank-you" note. This card is a representation of how family ties continue to keep friends connected. Even during the most unimaginable times; being gently tossed back together.

A few of Carol's samplings are now published and complete. Enjoy her writings and use this book as encouragement to complete your own dreams. I am thankful Carol has included me on this segment of her journey.

Many Blessings,

Antoinette M. Baker, MSM
Instructor, Author, Inspirational Speaker

THE LORD'S PRAYER

Our Father who art in heaven,
Hallowed be thy name;
Thy kingdom come;
Thy will be done on earth
As it is in heaven.

Give us this day our daily bread;
And forgive us our trespasses as we
forgive those who trespass against us;

And lead us not into temptation,
but deliver us from evil.
For thine is the Kingdom,
and the power, and the glory, forever.

Amen

PROLOGUE

Dear Toni,
    This card is actually one of my sister Delores' cards, as she left a drawer-full of future appropriate messages.
    The irony of it all is that we *really* met on my sister Juanita's doorsteps. This is where meaningful conversations made me aware of your present to me, my last chance!
    I have procrastinated long past any inspirational opportunities. Taking it all in stride.
    Today is the first day of autumn or for some, the last rose of summer. I am so excited!

Very Warm Regards,
Carol Alexander-Morgan

PART 1

LOVE RELATIONSHIPS

STRIPPED NAKED

I'm not a woman anymore.
My youth and spirit's gone.
I do just what I have to do
I'm merely looking on.

I'm unattractive, unadorned
Inadequate at best.
I cannot pull myself together
I am so depressed.

I cannot shake this feeling
It has haunted me so long.
I think back to the days
When I would sing happy a song.

There's not much to look forward to.
For me it seems too late.
I met a man so negative
It soon became my fate.

MUMBLE JUMBLE

Some fellows use a lot Mumble Jumble
To skirt the facts of which they cannot deal,
You tire, when you hear their same old story
Especially when, they know just how you feel.

You wonder why the same old bull revisits
When you threw it out the door the other day.
But someday then, you're forced to play the "heavy"
As the same old crap keeps getting in the way.

It is just because you love them, that you listen.
Still hoping that they'll change in time to keep…
The remnants of the romance from regressing,
Losing ground, and losing hope, and losing sleep.

LAUGHING STOCK

She tried to shun the moment
When she knew he'd go too far.
She tried to keep the pain away
That left an ugly scar.

She often felt belittled
And she let him know the score.
She fought it on the outside,
But, he brought it to her door.

Her pain just will not go away.
No matter how she tries.
She wished that day had never come.
And simply wants to die.

She felt humiliated,
Disappointed and disgraced.
She wished he'd screwed off in the dark,
Than frolicked in her face.

SWEET NOTHINGS

I'm looking for a friend to have a deep conversation with.
He needs to have great charm and intellect.
Einstein won't do, nor Greenspan; Shakespeare nor Cicero
I just need common sense and sweet respect.

I'm looking for a friend whose sensibilities
Are groomed for someone's cause besides his own,
So when he tells a joke it's truly funny.
Not just a chance to throw a verbal stone.

Who shuns the chance to put his foot so deeply in his mouth,
Regurgitating comments (as a pun).
The question is, the prime intent – he cast them out.
While aiming, picking me to be the one.

EMOTIONAL ROLLER COASTER

We've had our ups, but many downs
Transparent in our faces.
The laughs that seemed unending, now
Are frequently, evasive.

We've tried to throw the towel in,
But dread the repercussions.
Starting over, loneliness
And long drawn out discussions.

It all seems so unfortunate,
A tragic metaphor.
A counterfeit exterior,
To camouflage the score.

The plus and minus qualities.
The losses and the gains.
The benefits and detriment
The sorrow and the pain.

The mounting, double negatives
That greatly tips the scale,
Till all is lost, a graven cost.
This love was doomed, to fail.

The values were unequal,
Yet, we tried to make it work.
Now all that's left are memories,
Of every time…it hurt.

ROAD RAGE

We left as darkness settled into the daylight
His moody manner showed upon his face,
I never thought, that at **this** stage he'd grumble
Or let the devil, get back in this place.

The ride would take forever, in this fashion
The trend we set, so many years ago.
We just can't seem to get it all together
The argumentative frequency, won't slow.

It seems to grow momentous over nothing.
At least, when all is done, we will forget,
The argument itself, but not the subject.
We've said some things that both of us regret.

And now the ride continues in deep silence.
The short vacation promises to be,
An uphill battle, constantly repairing
The road that seems a bleak, eternity.

ROCKING CHAIR REFLECTIONS

At sixty, I feel fortunate to climax!
Especially when the tears swell in my eyes.
I never thought that I would think, "I'm all that".
In fact, it really caught me by surprise.

I raise my legs, I twist and shout.
The passion just goes on.
The next day when I think of it,
I sing a happy song.

A dear friend says that, that alone
Is worth more than all else.
That when you find your soul mate
You can start to think of self.

A perfect number sixty-nine,
The missionary style.
A pair of lips in harmony,
And breasts that always smile.

I won't complain of other things.
But, focus as I should,
On what my mate does so damn well!
Not other things he could.

THE MISSING LINK

I tidy up around the house.
My car is nice and clean.
I have some money in the bank.
I always make the scene!
I dress the part! I *look* that way.
I seek the current trends.
My status ranges equal to
Some of my **finest** friends.

I'm pretty nice. (You may think twice.)
(Excuse me if I boast)
As some I've seen, (and some might say)
More affable than most.
I've got a man, you understand.
I'm virtually at ease.
And yet, with all the things I have,
I still can't find true peace.

The emptiness is painful still
That permeates my mind.
The doubts and fears, the guilt, the tears
Are never far behind.

The *"missing link"* is quite distinct
I feel it in my soul.
There cannot be fulfillment then,
Until, I've been made whole.

'Till I put my trust in Jesus
Where His mercies never cease…
I'll be comforted in knowing
I have found that missing peace.

RUDE AWAKENING

I thought my life would be secure.
I thought I'd reach the age.
When life's big bowl of cherries
Would have taken center stage.

I knew there would be ups and downs
And flaws for all to see.
But, I didn't plan this party
Where the joke would be on me.

I thought that I would be admired
And envied for my joy.
The carefree life, the confidence,
And graciousness employed.

But, then this nightmare came to pass
I couldn't turn around…
My man on front street with a tramp
And I, looked like a clown.

HURDLING THE HILL

I'd like to think, I look the same
Each year that I get older.
But if I act the way I feel,
They'll say that I'm just bolder.

I run and shout, I laugh and cry.
My life's the same as yours.
The paths we tread are similar.
I've just gone 'round before.

Each strand of gray is paid in full.
I have some aches and pains.
But I feel good, each time I hear
The younger ones complain.

Though getting old, is something new,
The confidence I feel.
Is stamped with God's good graces.
That propels me over the hill.

CHOICES

Some women tolerate abuse
Or beatings every day.
The mind control is endless,
Based on what their man might say.

They stumble through the sleepless nights
As tears wash down their face.
The hurt inside, can no more hide,
Their picture of disgrace.

The feelings of belittlement,
Of blame and accusations.
Cast with ugly, raging sounds.
The roar of indignation.

They feel that it could be their fault.
The guilt just never ends.
They failed to nurse the whims of one
Who called themselves, their friend.

F.U.C.K. IS A FOR-BETTER WORD
(4-L)

(<u>F</u>riendship <u>U</u>nderstanding <u>C</u>onsideration <u>K</u>indness)
<u> 1   2   3   4</u>

If you think your man does love you,
But, he just won't let it show,
He's too busy fraternizing
With some stranger, friend or Ho.

Disrespect is all you're given,
He just ***will not*** treat you right.
Is this what you have accepted
Expectations out of sight?

Have the put-downs made you smaller,
Have you lost your sense of self?
Are your plans and dreams a riddle,
Have you placed them on the shelf?

Don't forget. Use ultimatums!
Hold it back, don't give it up.
Don't be scared he'll find another.
Don't give in to shallow bluff.

And **IF** he finds another
Could it be, he has before?
You deserve a life that's better.
Hasten to the nearest door.

If he cares, he'll reconsider,
All the pain he's put you through.
If you simply overlook it,
He will walk all over you.

You must hold him to the fire,
Just in case he hasn't heard…
If he wants to have *your* body
Fuck is one for-"Better" word!

RESPECTFULLY RETIRED

My days on Eight West Doan are through.
As memories flood my mind,
It seems that any moment, now…
It's all a dream…I'll find.

I've had some laughs, I've had some tears.
I've even had some fights.
I hope that I'll be seen as one,
Who stood for what is right.

So many people come to mind
Who've made me feel real good.
Some close relationships I've have,
And some misunderstood.

This phase of life has been unmatched
And worthy of this note…
I'll miss you terribly my friends.
So in this poem I wrote…

A wish that all God's blessings
Will reach you from the sky.
To keep you always looking up,
It's hard…to say good-by!

A PERSONAL POEM
(To Freddie Lee)

I woke up on my birthday
At the age of sixty-five.
I never dreamed that I would feel
So very much alive.

I didn't think my life with you
Would be so sweet at last.
Sometimes I let my memories
Bring up a stressful past.

But God…because we've asked Him
Made our union strong and true.
I am so glad to be your wife.
I'm still in love with you.

"AGE IS JUST A NUMBER (OF THINGS)"

You age each day and find a new affliction.
A bump or knot that wasn't there before.
A stiffness in the knees, a new addiction.
A nest of pills, you count on more and more.

Your body aches, your back is bent, you stumble.
Just getting off the bed, from restless sleep.
Your speech is slurred, or somewhat slowed, you mumble.
You climb the stairs that now seem very steep.

Ah, life is grand. It's just the aging process.
Your stool is hard, you make a dash to tinkle.
Your mind rewinds, the overload of senses.
Yet exercise can't change your veins or wrinkles.

So on you go, no sadness or resentment.
Just go on gracefully. Don't stand in line.
Remember this, to give you some contentment...
Each living soul will share this, too, in time.

STICKS AND STONES

Some people love to signify
And then call it a joke.
Sometimes an argument ensues
With just the one who spoke.

The person speaking seems to feel,
Superior in some way.
And so they pick the weakest point
To "make the other's day".

You'd think they'd know, or should expect
The one they're picking on…
Would then defend their posture,
Or position as a pawn.

In order for the joke to work
(Less it should fall on you,)
The laughs should come from everyone.
Of course, the victim, too.

No one should feel uneasy.
Or be planted on the spot.
What gives the right, to start a fight?
Your shit, is not that hot.

"TEAR TODAY, GONE TOMORROW"

He only saw a single tear
That trickled down her face.
He didn't recognize her pain
Or feelings of disgrace.

He thought that everything was fine.
He made it through the door.
It didn't seem that she was mad.
Or that she's keeping score.

He knew she'd reconsider, all
The pain he'd put her through.
And soon, she would forgive him.
So that they, would start anew.

It only was a single tear…
It couldn't hurt so much.
No claims nor confrontation.
Though, she couldn't stand his touch.

He never got the message.
Nor the writing on the wall.
It wasn't just a single tear…
That represented all.

It didn't tell the story, and
In fact, it's never shone…
The helplessness of one small tear
Upon a face of stone.

And so the chapter's ended, now
As anyone would fear.
There was no credibility
Assigned, to one small tear.

HOPELESS

I think it's best for us to part.
Before this hate invades my heart.
Before I wish you far away.
Then wished I'd never seen this day.

Before my energy is lost.
Before I suffer major cost,
Of losing softness in my soul
While gradually becoming cold.

Before I lose my hope and zest,
I feel it just might be the best.
Although it hurts for me to go.
Each day we hurt each other so.

The time has come when we must part.
But, always know you're in my heart.
Before I wish you far away.
And wished I'd never seen this day.

GO GENTLY

I never thought I'd let you in my life again.
I cried so much the day you went away.
And even though I thought I'd never let you go
This time, I never wanted you to stay.

Because I know those same old hurts return again.
And long before it's time enough to heal…
Those same old bleeding heart wounds, I sustained before.
That gloom of devastation that I feel.

Go gently with me please, this time I beg you.
Return the sweetness love always intends.
I'm only asking kind consideration.
Enough to give my heart a chance to mend.

GAS MASK

I stayed…or went back to the devil.
Persuaded by tears of remorse.
Blindsided by phony contrition
Intended to stave off divorce.

Instead of me seeking a counselor
Or running for fear of my life…
I stayed…or went back for the children
No matter the hardships or strife…

One night I was worn from the fighting
In horror, I hollered his name…
I rose from the bed, and found open…
The gas jets, but minus the flame…

GRATEFUL

(Dedicated to my husband, Freddie Lee)

Today at nearly eighty
Looking back across the years
Sitting at my kitchen table
Feeling free of pain and tears…

I am grateful for each moment
Good or bad, I won't complain
God has kept me through the trials
Through the losses and the gains.

Asleep behind the wheel one night
I got up off the ground.
From plowing into several poles
God never let me down.

Another time my car was hit
While on my way back to work
It was early in the morning
I was very much alert.

They cut me from the vehicle
And placed me on the cart…
I thought it was the end of me
Instead it was the start.

The next few years I met my mate.
I cannot underscore
The journey to this moment…For,
I could not love him more!

We thank God for protecting us
We speak with one accord…
For blessing our relationship,
We really Love the Lord!

PART 2

RELATIONSHIP WITH GOD

MY PRAYER
BECAUSE HE LOVES ME STILL

My soul was lost without you, Lord.
My life is disarray.
My morals shot to pieces, while
I sought to have my way.

My life was void of solid peace.
No comfort could I find,
In trusting mortals, mere like me,
With wretched states of mind.
A day disorganized, dismayed.
Enthusiasm spent,
On childish dreams and foolish schemes.
No yearning to repent.

Then, Lord, You laid your hand on me,
And helped me find my way.
I now proclaim the victory
And live for you each day.

Lord, thank you for your mercy.
Use me to do your will.
To ask the sinner lost in shame,
Who else would love us, still?

FRIENDLY AVICE

When God's mercy saves your life in constant turmoil,
And you soon forgot His pardon, for your crime…
You go on, then, repeating all your old ways.
But, you'll need Him once again, from time to time.

When you think you have it made, although He helped you.
You forget the time may come, when hell breaks through.
And no matter how much time is spent in praying…
You'll remember, and you'll know your time is due.

Then one day, you'll remember, when you're down and out
When you've blown that chance, that may not come again.
You'll be sorry, and you'll ask the Lord to save you.
When you feel, that you don't even have a friend.

As your friend, I think it's critical to tell you,
That it may be detrimental to your health.
Do not let your life destruct. He will heal you with His touch.
What He offers in return is peace and wealth.

PITFALLS

Take me back to where we started,
To the writing on the wall.
How'd I miss my mother's warning?
All I saw was cute and tall.

All I saw was cream and honey.
Focused only on the best.
Hardly ever paid attention
To the other glaring mess.

All the little digs and drama
Shuffling all around my feet.
Suffering pain, just like my Mama,
As the history repeats.

If I just, had called on Jesus…
And I weren't too blind to see…
That until **He** picks my partner,
He's the only man for me.

YOUNG AND FOOLISH

I've done some things throughout my life
Of which I'm not so proud.
Some secrets, now, lie very still.
And some, just shout out loud.

I've hurt, without intention,
Thinking mostly of myself.
In search of happiness I placed,
My values on the shelf.

Intent on worldly treasures,
I gave little to the Lord.
I traded peace for pleasures,
That my soul could not afford.

I look back now through aging wrinkles
At the life I shun,
And now discern the phrase that ***"Youth Is wasted, on the young."***

HELP ME TO BE STILL

Lord, thank you for this precious gift.
I owe it all to you.
I kneel so seldom in your name,
I'm anxious to be through.
I fumble for the words to say,
That's worthy of your love.
I'm struggling for the perfect term.
It's me, I'm thinking of.

I'm worried if I'll sound contrite.
I wonder why I'm bound.
This bondage, surrendered,
Keeps my feet from solid ground.
I worry over other's thoughts.
And what they think of me.
And if my gift is good enough,
To set my bondage free.

I feel so guilty deep inside.
For where I ought to be.
You could have chosen someone else.
Instead, you're blessing me.
I feel so restless, void of peace.
I cannot concentrate.
I can't fulfill my purpose…
I need you, to keep me straight.

I don't deserve this blessing
For I haven't taken time.
To worship you, and praise your name.
It's me, I have in mind.
Lord, make my motives Christ-like,
In everything I do.
Despite my good intentions,
Please reassure they're true.

Lord, bless this gift, refresh me
And use me to your will.
Lord turn me up, and shake shelf out.
And help me, to be still.

OUT OF THE ARK

Sometimes I just don't call you, Lord.
Although I know you're there.
I feel so empty and ashamed.
So much…that I don't dare.

I've shut you out because I know
The things that you require.
And I can hardly measure up.
Though, it's my heart's desire.

I just can't seem to get it right.
I struggle to pursue…
Illusive dreams, by my own means.
Instead of seeking you.

Lord, pierce me with your spirit.
And shake my mind of dust.
That clutters as it gathers, and
Obliterates my trust.

LORD, strengthen me, increase my faith.
And make me not ashamed,
To seek you in my sorrow
And cry out loud your name.

I MUST CALL UPON THE LORD

When temptation violates my precious safety zone,
I must call upon the Lord to set me free.
I'm no longer in control of lustful feelings.
They surround and tickle every bone in me.

When I know what's right, but want to bask in daydreams,
And can't control the urges that I feel…
I call upon my mighty loving Savior.
For He will help me. Only He can heal.

He heals my spirit lost in sinful pleasures…
My soul entrenched in loose and foolish play,
My wanton passion, tugging at my heart strings,
That tempting nag that will not go away.

But, His ***power,*** omnipresent, everlasting
Can obliterate confusion evermore.
If I call Him every morning, every evening,
And at nighttime…He will hasten to my door.

GOD'S GIFT

God gave me such a lovely gift.
He gave me words so say.
He gave me passion with the truth
That might help light the way.

He gave me courage, guts and brawn.
To stand for what is right.
He gave me health and strength and love,
Support to win the fight.

I owe to him a heart that's pure.
A spirit kind and true,
Who seeks his footsteps day by day.
These urgings, I must do!

I must speak out! I've words to say.
His mercy *never* fails!
If we have faith, and trust in Him,
We'll know, that "It Is Well".

THE SET-UP

There are those afraid, like I was
To surrender to the Lord.
The fear of being tested
Was too painful to afford.

I knew I really loved Him.
But, the way I let Him know,
Was to take His love for granted
All those blessings He bestowed.

I ignored His gentle calling
Hoping not to be too late.
Lacking joy, but needing courage.
Still resisting, so I'd wait.

Then at last I heard the message,
That when troubles come our way.
We're the victims of a "set-up"
God's preparing "better" days.

He will make us, mold us, cleanse us,
As we kneel before His Throne
He didn't bring us here, this far
To leave us all alone.

Oh ye, therefore, be encouraged.
Trust your life in His great hands.
He has made you. He will save you.
He will change you – He's **"The Man"**.

WALKING IN THE REIGN

The leaves came down in great majestic splendor
And through the woods the rain fell when I trod.
Then high above the fence, between the trees. There,
I felt, upon my face, the reign of God.

The rain conducted symphonies – the craft of God
As He composed, selections graced His throne,
To let us know that if we yield **our** will for **His**
There's beauty that we may have never known.

The leaves, in silent rhythm, spiraled downward
The tree lined picket fence stood straight and tall,
The pale blue skies recovered over dark gray clouds
God's majesty turned summer into fall!

RAINDANCE

I love the rain upon my roof.
The rhythm and the beat.
The dancing drops upon my window,
Are a sweet retreat.

Inducing mellow memories
Reflections of my mind.
The jungle beat of distant drums
Now softly taps in time.

So peacefully submitted
A glorified refrain…
I love to write beneath the skylight
On the day it rains.

REMISSION

I lost my way while seeking God.
I didn't take the time…
To search Him out completely
And to make Him truly mine.

I knew He was the Father
And I knew He was the Son.
I knew that all my blessings were
From nothing I had done.

I took Him so for granted
He, who came to give me life.
Abundantly accepting it,
But not the pain or strife.

I couldn't grasp His fullness
Or earnestly commit,
To give my life completely
For my lifestyle didn't fit.

I often failed to say my prayers
Or bless the food I ate.
I didn't ask for answers
For I knew I couldn't wait.

I didn't mean to hurt the Lord.
He's been so good to me.
I beg forgiveness for my sins.
And those of Calvary.

JESUS ON MY MIND

When I concentrate on Jesus
All my cares just roll away
When I understand His greatness,
And His mercies everyday…

I'll discern a bigger picture
With a panoramic view
Of the Savior, who's been there for me
Who's surely there for you.

When I realize all my blessings
From the High and Holy one
I will know with great prospective
It's from nothing I have done.

That, alone, should make me wonder
How could I avoid a time…
Any chance to seek His presence
And to have Him on my mind.

HE WILL PROVIDE

The Presence of the Lord is all around me.
I feel it in my soul, both night and day.
I wonder why the Lord, chose to surround me?
When I have always sought to have my way.

When I need a "high", He sends my heart a message,
A song of joy to set my soul afire.
When I am low, He picks me up and keeps me.
Throughout the night, while I, in peace retire.

I slumber through the night in sweet fulfillment.
And wake with cheerful thoughts inside my head.
My day is going on in sweet remembrance…
Of all the words my Jesus ever said.

"Fear not my child, for I am with you always."
"Don't be afraid to give your life to me."
I asked the Lord to cleanse and make me over.
His word is true, for all the world to see.

PRAYER CHANGES THINGS

Sometimes, the load is heavy
And the day seems awfully long…
When you ponder over problems,
Weighing right against the wrong.

Just remember God **is** with you.
And **_He_** knows which way to go.
You can feel His tender mercies,
When He knows you need Him so.

His hand is always outstretched
Just to gently take you in.
He doesn't push, no pleading.
For, He just wants you to win.

The right way to the tree of life,
The butter for your soul,
The bread of life, the blood-stained wine
Your name signed on the role.

No matter what the problem is
You'll know that God is there.
If only _**you**_, will take the steps
To go to Him in prayer.

PART 3

FAMILY

"ROOSEVELT'S RECOVERY"

I stand, Almighty God, in humble quietness.
I see the mighty forest through the trees.
I reel in awe of your amazing splendor.
Your work unfinished, still defies belief.

Your mighty wondrous mercies are astounding.
For through it all, it's clear that you've begun…
Your cleansing powers…showers, on the faithful!
It's so illuminating in my son!

"SISTER-LOVE"
(Dedicated to and written for my greatest cheerleader –
my sister, Juanita Potts)

I've never stopped to say how much I love you.
You've helped me out, so many other ways.
Than anyone at all expects a sister
To sacrifice so much in bygone days.

And still you keep on giving any moment.
You're always looking for the dove of peace.
You pray for all, redeeming all transgressions.
The love is selfless, that you give, with ease.

It's not to say I'm blind to your shortcomings.
I recognize the gene that is my own.
It's just to say, you've been there, for me always.
And look at how the both of us have grown!

"WINGS OVER JORDAN"
(1982)

When my sister Joyce offered to pay my way to the Holy Land, I turned her down, twice; having no desire to go. Weeks later reluctantly, I agreed to go for her sake, so that she might have a compatible roommate. From the moment I said yes, my heart was heavy. Despite the encouragement of family, friends and co-workers, all wishing to be in my shoes. I thought, "What on earth am I going to do in the Holy Land for 11 days?" I couldn't even take any of those little funny, leisure-time cigarettes that elevate and magnify feelings.

Planning and preparing for a trip was something I looked forward to well in advance. This time I threw a suitcase together the night before and took the Greyhound to Cleveland to spend the night with my sister, Juanita. Her husband, Douglas, took us all to the airport the next morning. "Cheer up" Juanita said. "You're going to have a great time because you're not expecting anything."

Eighteen other people, all unknown to me, including the pastor who planned the tour, were waiting inside the airport. All with eager anticipation, and itineraries in hand. Joyce was in seventh heaven.

On the plane, I briefly looked over corresponding information Joyce had sent me, for the first time. I recalled she had given up the idea of encouraging me to wear a white dress to be baptized in the River of Jordan. She knew I wouldn't go if she continued to insist. I had been baptized at the age of nine; became a "Sunday-morning" Christian, considered myself a good person and was not ready to change my life. I was having a good time. Although I rarely prayed and took the time to thank God for His blessings in the manner that I should.

Somehow at the beginning of the fourteenth hour of flight on three planes, I knew someone else was in control of my destiny on this trip. God used a person on the tour, a strong vessel, to tell me about Jesus and all of His glories.

In Israel, thousands of miles from home, we followed the paths of Jesus; reading passages as they related to the places we stopped. In a little town where Jesus preached and prayed, I was baptized with twenty others in the River of Jordan, in slacks and a blouse.

The transition following my return home has not been a smooth one. But God has most assuredly seen me through my ups and downs. With the Lord ever present in my life, it is comforting and inspiring. He has allowed me a personal relationship, unknown to me before. He is able to keep me on a natural high. No stimulants needed.

Day by day He directs the circumstances of my life that I may come to recognize and know Him. Also, that I may seek His guidance to fulfill my purpose in life, in service to Him. To God be the glory. I need Him to live my life for Him each day.

"I REMEMBER MAMA"

I remember mama
In her housedress made of plaid.
Her hair, an upswept velvet wave.
Her face was often sad.
Her eyes of blue sincerity,
Were hazel in the sun.
Angelic perseverance was
A victory, she had won.

Most memories though, were happy,
And she praised my written words.
I'm sure that they reminded her
Of some she'd often heard.
Her father was a preacher,
With strong views of loving care.
A blueprint to salvation.
An instrument to share.

A map of humble righteousness.
A draft, a guarantee.
A bible for God's followers
And sinners, too, like me.
If only she could see me now,
And call my name out loud.
Then, she could see what God has done
And she would be so proud.

Although, there's not much chance of that,
I guess she always knew...
That one day I would see the light,
And raise my voice up, too.
To sing the praise of Jesus
And share His written words,
To some who may not know Him,
And those who haven't heard.

"MY FATHER, THE FUROR" (der führer)

I shuddered in my bed when all around me,
Were clumps of blankets, hiding little souls.
Reduced to fear and clear intimidation.
Afraid to peek out in the night or cold.

The footsteps on the stairs were loud and frightening.
The force and fury of a drunken beast…
Would shatter all my dreams and start us crying.
He'd pull us from the bed by hands and feet.

He dragged our mother screaming, to the bathroom.
A forceful hold, her long hair in his grip.
She'd always cry, "What have I done?" in sorrow.
To say more, would ensure a busted lip.

His drunken manner mocked, accused and cursed us.
He lined us up, according to our age.
The youngest, I was seated next to mother.
As he destroyed us, with consuming rage.

This terrifying ordeal was consistent,
Expected two or three times, every week.
At three or four, the wee hours the of morning.
The Furor left his mark on Mama's cheek.

He blamed us for his problems and his anger.
A raging bull who needed no excuse,
To justify his horrifying actions.
His power rose, with physical abuse.

Alas, those days have ended, but the memory,
Indelibly remains in scars and tears.
Forever deeply rooted in my psyche,
It rears its ugly head across the years.

"MY FIRST CHILD…
MY ONLY DAUGHTER"
(1959 - 1988)
(Written in 2004)

Michelle was still trying to find herself at age 29 when she was killed with a gun, by an older man she knew. Michelle was on her way to reunite with her fiancé, a man of her own age, who was busy preparing for their Memorial Day Celebration.

Michelle had great potential. But she left this earth before she could prove it to her family and friends; in the way which she would have wanted to. Her talent and educational skills placed her at the top of her data processing class. She was in the process of enjoying her life and her new future.

Many factors went into shaping Michelle's existence; as with all of us, as well. But when your child dies before you do, it is probable that you ask yourself… "What could I have done differently?" Most likely, now, you have all of the answers, but you didn't see it that way then. Or, you weren't able to change things for some reason. Or…you just could not have known.

That measure of guilt prompted my awareness that my daughter's murderer might one day be a patient on the hospital's prison unit where I worked as a nurse. Could I avenge my daughter's senseless killing?

It would not be a difficult task to accomplish by the way things were set up on our floor. Would I feel worse if I didn't? Should I abandon logic and values in order to feel a motherly sense of devotion that I may not have expressed before, in a way that she needed?

Those feelings were a part of me every day when I looked at the roster of patients in our 27 bed unit at the OSU

Hospital Medical Center. It was for five years that I checked the board, dutifully, with no occurrences of his admission.

During the trial, the victim's impact statements by the family included an acknowledgment of my employer. But the red flags were not in place the day Troy Cameron slipped through the cracks of the system.

It was 1993. I was charge nurse that day. It was my duty to assign the next patient coming from the SICU to another nurse. It was an extraordinarily busy day for all of the staff; so I took the report, myself, from the transferring nurse. At the end of the report, stunned, I reconfirmed his first name and age.

To my horror, the measly five to fifteen year sentence had taken its toll on the man, who was even sixteen years *my* senior. Now he needed our unit as a step-down, just before he would be released from prison. What was I to do?

I went to the Captain in corrections to see if they would intervene in the transfer of that patient to our unit. It was customary to transfer all satellite room patients to the medical-surgical prison unit as soon as their condition warranted, for safety and economical reasons.

The Captain did his best, but was unable to change policy for this one occasion. The patient's doctor, upon knowing of the situation said, "I'll do one better. I'll send the 'B' back down to the 'fence'."

The next time I heard the name "Troy Cameron" was when one of my best friends, Pat, another nurse, called me at home. She was working the night duty shift on our unit. It was 3:00am when my phone rang.

"Wake up" she said. "Don't be afraid. What is the name of the man who killed your daughter?" I responded, "Troy Cameron." "Don't come, in the morning. I called the supervisor who has a replacement for you. She will have the inmate off the floor in a few hours."

Pat, who attended my daughter's funeral in Cleveland, Ohio in 1988, after 16 straight hours of work, was more than concerned about my welfare. I could hear the anxiety in her voice as she struggled to juggle her charge duties with this personal problem involving me.

Now, that it had reopened old wounds, I thought, how long was this man going to impact my life and the life of my family and friends who cared about me and Michelle. It also impacted my co-workers, who gave wonderful and unbiased care, which was one of my biggest worries.

Pat said, "He was getting out soon to live with his daughter and his grandchildren." My heart sunk...Immediately my mind went back to the baby girl Michelle had when she was sixteen. We gave my first born grandchild to Children Services for adoption, at birth in 1975; because this is what Michelle wanted. Baby girl Ann, would be 29 years old at the time of this writing. We have not seen her since her birth.

The next time I said the name, "Troy Cameron", Pat called me while she was at work on Halloween Eve, a few weeks later. "What's the name of the man who killed your daughter?" In a zombie-like manner, I could hardly fix my lips again to say... "Troy Cameron". "He's dead!" she said. "He came into ER. He coded...and died."

(Dedicated with much love to Patricia Zidar whose father's birthday is the same day Michelle was killed. Without whom I would never know the final circumstances of the convicted Cameron, the killer of my child.)

MISSING MICHELLE

I'd give anything to have her back with us again.
My hopes and spirit died with her, that day.
I have pondered on my many flaws and failures
Thinking, what if life had been another way.

What if I had given more of what she needed?
What if I'd prepared and dared to make her stay.
Would the same destructive circumstance surround her?
Could her life have made a turn, the other way?

Would my conscience then, stay warm with every heartbeat?
Could the happy recollections of my mind,
Be a comfort to my soul that's ever longing
For a moment, to reverse the hands of time.

(August 9, 1959 – May 27, 1988)

A PARENT'S PRAYER

We may not have a chance to choose
The way our children grow,
The kind of people they become
The places they may go.

We pray with all our might that
They will find the peaceful things.
The joy and all the happiness
An earnest heart can bring.

We wish that life's adversities
Will somehow pass them by.
The heartaches we can't shield them from,
The pain that makes them cry.

And life will all its mysteries
The bitter and the sweet,
Shall test them, till the strong survives
As others meet defeat.

We pray, Oh God, we waste no time
In wishing cares away.
Replace, instead, in us the zeal
To deal with life, each day.

FAMILY PICTURE

I'm so much like my family.
(Though, I really think, I'm not.)
I see myself in each of them
I come from good, fine stock.

But, one peculiar habit…
That annoys me to no end,
Is not justified, until I'm told
"You're like that, too, my friend!"

Now, when I get too picky
And think that they should change.
I just look into the mirror,
And then, call them by **my** name.

So, if you have a family feud.
Don't tear them all apart.
Rather, dwell upon their goodness, then,
And keep that trait in heart.

SOUL FOOD

I love my family more and more
The smaller that it gets.
I realize what they mean to me
Great times, I can't forget.

I see them at the church or store
Or in the neighborhood
At family picnics, funerals,
And places that I should.

I mingle, laugh and say, "What's up?"
But rarely think to say.
"I love you, uncle, cousin, niece
I'm glad you passed my way."

Sometimes, they may think I don't care
Or really give a hoot.
Let me refresh my love to them
And fertilize my roots.

A RAINBOW FOR ROBYN

So graceful in her style and form
While standing tall and strong.
Sometimes an air of mystery
As she would pass along.

An independent nature yet
While giving God His due.
The ultimate, uplifting praise
That she would share with you.

She never bragged or boasted
Of the attributes she owned.
Although her manifested deeds
Were clear and brightly shone.

Her military service to our country
Was its best.
But, as an organ donor
She surpassed the greatest test.

What sacrifice is higher,
On the metaphoric shelf.
Than of giving life to others,
More than thinking of yourself?

Her humor was indelible
A hand she often dealt.
Her gift to us, to lessen,
All the helplessness we felt.

She felt God's Holy Spirit
Cradled in His loving arms.
Accepting all that came her way…
No fear of dread nor harm.

So though the breadth of air has ceased
Her memory lingers on.
But when the child precedes the mom,
The pain is never gone.

What can be said to ease the pain,
To make the days seem bright again?
A fallen star has graced our path
And risen to a higher class.

Her utmost…unrelenting,
As she held on to the rod.
Fully lucid in her weakness,
Clearly showed the strength of God!

Knowing that her days were ending.
No regrets and no remorse.
Fly away our Darling Robyn
To God's Great Celestial Shores!

Lovingly Aunt Carol

SUMMERS ON THE FARM
(Dedicated to Aunt Gladys and Uncle George with much love)

When looking back through childhood,
IT IS FAR BEYOND A DOUBT.
That our wonderful experiences
In ***Farmville*** stand right out.

Our Aunt and Uncle took us in
So dutiful and brave.
Four cousins, who except for one
Weren't worthy of their praise.

The three of us would try their skills
Of parenting us all.
We'd stretch their patience mightily
'Til Uncle George grew tall.

Aunt Gladys just went round and round
A smile still on her face.
When I think back, on our childhood,
I think…***how we loved that place***.

The horse and cart, the pigs and hogs…
The goats and chickens fed.
The crops we picked to compliment
Aunt Gladys' homemade bread.

The winding roads, the choo-choo trains
The house upon the hill.
These precious memories stokes the coals
And lingers, warmly, still.

Yes summers spent in Farmville
With Aunt "GLAD" and Uncle George
Are among the things we cherish
In the memories that are stored.

FAMILY TREE

It's bittersweet this moment
As my childhood dream comes true
I have squandered good intentions
Then it came "out of the blue"!

My siblings couldn't cheer for me
The last one's gone away.
And I, the last of seven
Felt that happened yesterday
.
But------God,
Whose plans determine
What the future is for me.
Will decide if I am leaning
On the Holy family tree.

"WHAT GOES AROUND"

Sometimes we think an old cliché
Is banter, trite, but true.
They say whatever goes around,
Will come right back to you.

Especially, if **you** sent it there.
Although, you may not see…
That, the same old thing "I hated"
Will sure return to me.

"I hated Mom, I hated Dad."
You hear that all the time.
From cultures all around the world.
Exclusive in their minds.

What happens in that process
From their venom-flowing lips
Manifests an ugly feature,
With no reassuring grip.

It reeks an unattractiveness
That's plastered on their face
Relinquishing all reasons
To take that person's place.

There's no way of resolving,
Through an artificial way...
The years of scorn and hatred.
That had mounted day by day.

Ignoring clear conditions...
Commanded from above.
How can we see our brother
As a person, not to love?

Somehow it seems to happen,
That the one they hate the most
Is the one they'll pattern after...
Resurrecting tired ghosts.

PART 4

COUNTRY

A SOLDIER'S SORROW

A soldier stepped down from the train
And hurried to a phone.
Impatiently, he called his folks
So glad, to be back home.

"Hello" he said, "Mom, this is Dave
Yes, Mom, I'm home at last."
He then remarked, how long it's been.
How slowly, time had passed.

He clutched the phone much tighter,
And then begin to add…
"I'd like to bring a friend with me
To stay awhile, ask Dad."

"Of course, dear, that's just fine with me.
And Dad will feel the same."
"Oh Mom," Dave added, cautiously…
My friend, in fact, in lame."

"Oh Dave," she said, somewhat refrained,
"No that would never do.
He'd only be a burden, so out of place here, too.
And, then, what would our dear friends think
And what might others say?
At parties, trips and socials,
He'd just be in the way.

If only he were just alright,
Then all would be just grand.
But, can't you see the way things are?
Dear, won't you understand?"

He turned to leave. He wiped his face.
His brow was worn and beat.
He took the crutch beside him…
And hobble down the street.

DON'T WAIT

Never miss a chance to say, "I love you."
Always keep that promise, if you can.
Treasure every moment spent together
Often, hold the other person's hand.

Value all the pleasures that you cherish
Always keep them warm inside your heart,
Count the many ways to make one happy.
Life is short - and all too soon, we part.

Give that loved one, much consideration.
Plan each day as though it soon could end.
Hold them tightly! Keep the faith. Be faithful!
Say the words, "I love you," to your friend.

"THE SHELTER"

On frigid nights, the homeless stand in lines around the corner.
All, waiting for a number from a can.
They're praying that their digits fall below the legal limit.
The shelter hopes the others understand.

Rejection, disappointment in a circle long endured.
Humiliation smacks them in the face.
An icy sting, a bitter ring, for those still unsecured.
A wake up call, that there is no more space.

Some turn away and make their stay at camps around the city,
Beneath the bridge, a cardboard box, or hole.
The sad effects of life gone wrong is never, ever pretty.
The season sends its ugly, bitter cold.

Be strong, my homeless brother, take your plight to city hall.
Then take it to the Master in the sky.
And many, who would disregard, their pleading earnest call,
Could say, but for the grace of God, go I.

HEATHER TAKE US HIGHER
(Killed during protest against white nationalists)

The world just came to know this gal
And feisty she must be.
With righteous indignation
Over hurt and cruelty.

Her life was short but reaching far
Her message loud and clear.
"If you're not outraged," you don't know
The reasons you must fear.

"If you're not outraged," Heather says…
By things so clearly wrong.
"You haven't paid attention"
Or you simply go along.

We must speak out "for Heaven's sake!"
For those we do admire.
"When they go low, we must go high"
Dear Heather, take us higher!

(4th v 3rd line – First Lady Michelle Obama)

When I think of Heather, I am reminded of the prayer of Saint Francis of Assisi; "Lord make me an instrument of thy peace." "Where there is hatred, let me show love…"

P.O.W.

Under the darkest conditions
Held on the coldest terrain
Lost among foes in their killing fields
'Mid thunder – and lightening – and rain.

Tortured and battered by enemies
Braving their daring demands,
Hope against hope for recovery
Praying for God's helping hand.

Then suddenly, sirens for safety
Boomed loudly and trumpets were heard
Confirming the white flag of freedom
As angels, appeared, on God's word.

"Fear not, my child for I am with you always".
The solders rose, who stood among the dead,
"My rod and staff will comfort you." And quickly,
Our soldier boys remembered, what God said.

SWEET MARY

Mary O'Cain of Virginia, has
A record that anyone can see
Her life was one of blessing folks,
In her community.

Her beauty was external
From her heart of gold within.
In her sickness, was her passion
Just to serve, the church again.

She was faithful, as exemplified
A doer of God's word
A servant unto others
In the special way, she served.

They say that in her market
She would often take the time
To plant a gift in someone's bag
That they, at home, would find.

Yes, Mary of LOVE ZION
Had a heart as pure as gold
She made all her interventions
Leave a warm and tender glow.

We miss you so, sweet Lady "O"
Our tears pour down like the rain.
But God, whose hand has picked you up,
Has vanquished all your pain!

Mary, tell them not to weep, and
Tell your family not to moan.
Tell the saints, you've gone to Heaven
To your everlasting home!

FELLOW FRIENDS

I've always made an effort to accommodate my friends.
No matter what they asked of me, I'd take it to the end.
I'd give them things I didn't need to keep all to myself.
I tried uplifting spirits. Always thought of someone else.

I always tried to compliment the things that they did well.
I'd never take for granted, that they'd know, if I don't tell.
I've been so very lucky, that some special friends I've made
Have treated me *"mo' better"*, and I'll take that to my grave.

It's really great to know someone who feels the way you do.
Whose special hospitality, you are invited to.
Who makes that special effort to the very dying end,
Of practicing their friendship. Just to keep the **best** of friends.

MEMORIES

We used to laugh and talk with you,
As good friends often do.
Share our problems, chew the fat,
And fry a fish or two.

Linger over memories
Of happy days gone by.
Talk of family, job and friends,
Laugh until we cry.

So sadly we will miss you,
As so painfully we part.
But we know we'll keep our memories fresh
And warm, inside our hearts.

HEROES-911

You are gone, but not forgotten
Though we barely knew your names.
Many innocent bystanders
Who received unwelcome fame.

So many unsung heroes.
By anyone's account.
A devastating tragedy
Too horrid, to surmount.

The cost of precious human life,
Can never be repaid. But,
The name of valor goes to you.
And at your grave, is laid.

LIGHTS OUT

He woke up crying in the dark wee hours.
In deep regret for all the wrong he'd done.
The shattered innocence of all his victims,
Resulted in the destiny, he'd won.

Somewhat relieved, his past, a distant memory
Lent safety, by the absence of the view.
A stained glass pane, obscuring; yet reflecting…
A picture of the violent world he knew.

He pondered on his evil deeds and failures.
A family trait that offered no excuse.
A meager life was thrust on him in childhood
A victim of incredible abuse.

This pattern of behavior was repeated.
The vicious cycle would be broken, soon.
The last descendant, of his line reported
To execution, yesterday, at noon.

MOUNTAIN OF EVIDENCE

Sock stains, blue-black fibers,
Lots of D.N.A.
Blood drops in the parlor.
Footprints all the way.

Hair in cashmere linings,
Fur flies in the air.
Fingerprints on envelopes,
Tracings on the stair.

Social implications.
Drama, as you please.
Evidence predictable,
Meets forensic needs.

Facts that prosecutors
Would kill to speak about.
But then there is the jury,
Who may still, find reasoned doubt.

INVASION OF PRIVACY

Not ever in his wild imagination,
Did he presume the trial would go this way.
Who'd ever think his sagging body image
Would dominate the T.V. screen each day?

He never visualized a pair of panties
Would be placed into our face, for all to see.
The private and the personal possessions
Of a lady who was stripped of dignity.

Who was stripped of her most private, inner moments
By a man who was supposed to be her friend.
But, who lost the reins he needed to control her
And felt that now, her life would have to end.

The incident was absolutely horrid.
How does a person think they have the right…
To take a life that interferes with their plans
And make that person vanish out of site.

Do you think that is was worth it now, defendant?
Is the outcome at this moment worth the cost?
The privacy and shattered lives of love ones
Are no measure, for the lovely lady, lost.

BIG BOY BLUE

We count on you to be there,
When we wake, afraid at night.
When others drink, and go too far
Or start a vicious fight.

We count on Blue to be there
When someone is acting mean,
Enough to steal possessions
Or to trespass on our scene.

We need them when our kids are lost.
For highway safety, too.
When we need help, or panic,
We are happy to see Blue.

The crime wave is increasing.
Many criminals at large.
Who else comes to our rescue?
That will be there, free of charge?

So if one apple spoils the bunch
That you cannot defend.
We thank you for your service,
And regard you as our friend.

Printed in Great Britain
by Amazon